I0466995

RAGINI

Mastering Affiliate Marketing

A STEP-BY-STEP GUIDE

TO BOOST YOUR INCOME

"Mastering YouTube Affiliate Marketing: A Step-by-Step Guide to Boost Your Income"

what readers can expect to gain

Here's what readers can expect to gain from "Mastering YouTube Affiliate Marketing: A Step-by-Step Guide to Boost Your Income":

- Proven strategies to effectively monetize your YouTube channel through affiliate marketing.

- Step-by-step guidance on setting up and optimizing affiliate campaigns tailored for YouTube.
- Insider tips on choosing the right affiliate programs and products to maximize earnings.
- Techniques to grow your audience and increase engagement while promoting affiliate offers.
- Real-world examples and case studies illustrating successful affiliate marketing on YouTube.
- Actionable insights to turn your YouTube passion into a sustainable income stream through affiliate partnerships.

Introduction

Certainly! Here's the introduction for your eBook "Mastering YouTube Affiliate Marketing: A Step-by-Step Guide to Boost Your Income" in British English:

Welcome to "Mastering YouTube Affiliate Marketing: A Step-by-Step Guide to Boost Your Income". In today's digital landscape, YouTube has evolved beyond a platform for entertainment into a powerful tool for generating income. Whether you're a seasoned content creator or just starting out, harnessing the potential of affiliate marketing on YouTube can significantly enhance your earnings and expand your audience reach.

This comprehensive guide is designed to equip you with the essential knowledge and practical skills needed to navigate the world of affiliate marketing effectively on YouTube. From understanding the fundamentals of affiliate marketing to implementing advanced strategies, each chapter provides clear, actionable steps supported by real-world examples and insights.

You'll discover how to identify profitable affiliate programs, create compelling content that converts, and optimize your channel for maximum engagement and revenue. Whether your goal is to supplement your current income or turn YouTube into a full-time career, this eBook will empower you to leverage affiliate marketing strategies that work.

Get ready to transform your passion for YouTube into a lucrative venture. Let's embark on this journey together and unlock the secrets to mastering YouTube affiliate marketing.

Index

Certainly! Here are 10 ways you can leverage affiliate marketing on YouTube to boost your income:

1. Create Engaging Reviews: Produce detailed reviews of products relevant to your audience's interests, embedding affiliate links in your video description.

2. Incorporate Tutorials: Offer step-by-step tutorials or demonstrations showcasing how products can solve common problems, with affiliate links for easy purchase.

3. Feature Product Comparisons: Compare various products within your niche, highlighting pros and cons to help viewers make informed decisions.

4. Promote Special Offers: Share exclusive discounts or limited-time offers available through affiliate partnerships, creating urgency for viewers to buy.

5.Use Call-to-Actions (CTAs): Encourage viewers to click on affiliate links by including clear CTAs in your video and description.

6.Collaborate with Brands: Partner with brands for sponsored content that includes affiliate links, ensuring alignment with your audience's interests.

7.Host Giveaways: Organize giveaways of affiliate-linked products, boosting engagement and incentivising viewer participation.

8.Create Evergreen Content: Produce timeless content that continues to attract views and generate affiliate income long after its initial upload.

9.Optimise SEO: Use relevant keywords and phrases in your video titles, descriptions, and tags to improve visibility and attract organic traffic.

10.Engage with Your Audience: Foster a loyal community by responding to comments, addressing viewer queries, and soliciting feedback to refine your affiliate marketing strategies.

CHAPTER NO. 1

Creating Engaging Reviews: A Comprehensive Guide to Boosting Affiliate Marketing on YouTube

Producing detailed product reviews is a powerful strategy to engage your audience and drive affiliate sales on YouTube. A well-crafted review not only informs and entertains but also builds trust, encouraging viewers to click on your affiliate links and make purchases. This guide will provide you with a step-by-step approach to creating engaging reviews, covering everything from preparation and content creation to optimization and promotion.

1. Understanding Your Audience

To create compelling reviews, it's crucial to understand your audience's interests and needs. Conduct thorough research to identify their preferences, pain points, and the type of products they are likely to purchase.

- **Audience Analysis:** Use YouTube Analytics to gain insights into your audience's demographics, interests, and viewing habits. This data will help you tailor your reviews to meet their expectations.
- **Community Engagement:** Engage with your viewers through comments, polls, and social media interactions. Ask them directly about the products they're interested in and the kind of reviews they find most helpful.

2. Choosing the Right Products

Select products that align with your niche and resonate with your audience. Your reviews will be more authentic and effective if you genuinely believe in the products you're promoting.

- **Relevance:** Choose products that are relevant to your channel's theme and audience's interests. For example, a tech channel should focus on gadgets and software, while a beauty channel should review cosmetics and skincare products.

- Quality: Ensure the products are of high quality and provide value to your viewers. Reviewing subpar products can damage your credibility and reduce trust in your recommendations.
- Diversity: Offer a mix of products, including high-end, mid-range, and budget options, to cater to a wider audience.

3. Preparing for the Review

Thorough preparation is key to delivering a comprehensive and engaging review. Gather all necessary information about the product and plan your review structure.

- Research: Research the product thoroughly, including its features, specifications, and user reviews. Understand its strengths and weaknesses to provide an informed opinion.
- Personal Experience: Use the product yourself to gain firsthand experience. This will allow you to share genuine insights and practical tips with your viewers.
- Script Writing: Write a script or outline for your review to ensure a smooth flow and cover all essential points. A well-structured script helps in delivering a coherent and engaging review.

4. Creating the Review Content

Now that you're prepared, it's time to create the review. Focus on producing high-quality content that is both informative and entertaining.

- **Introduction:** Start with a captivating introduction that grabs viewers' attention. Briefly introduce the product and explain why you chose to review it.
- **Unboxing (if applicable):** Show the unboxing process if the product is new. Highlight the packaging, included accessories, and first impressions. This adds an element of excitement and curiosity.
- **Detailed Review:** Provide a thorough review of the product, covering its features, performance, pros and cons, and your personal experience. Be honest and balanced in your evaluation.
  - **Features:** Describe the product's key features and how they compare to similar products. Use close-up shots to highlight important details.
  - **Performance:** Test the product in real-world scenarios and share your findings. For example, if reviewing a smartphone, demonstrate its camera quality, battery life, and user interface.
  - **Pros and Cons:** Discuss the product's strengths and weaknesses. This helps viewers make an informed decision and builds trust in your review.

- Use Cases: Provide examples of how the product can be used and who would benefit most from it. This helps viewers relate to the product and envision its value in their lives.
- Call to Action (CTA): Conclude your review with a strong CTA, encouraging viewers to click on the affiliate links in the video description. You can also invite them to leave comments, share their experiences, and ask questions.

5. Optimizing Your Video for SEO

SEO optimization is crucial to increase the visibility of your review and attract organic traffic. Implement these strategies to improve your video's search ranking.

- Title: Craft a compelling and keyword-rich title that accurately reflects the content of your review. For example, "In-Depth Review of the New iPhone 14 – Features, Performance, and User Experience."
- Description: Write a detailed video description, including relevant keywords and a summary of the review. Include affiliate links prominently and provide a brief disclaimer about your affiliate relationship.
  - Affiliate Links: Embed your affiliate links early in the description for easy access. Use trackable links to monitor clicks and conversions.

- Tags: Use relevant tags to help YouTube understand the content of your video and recommend it to the right audience. Include a mix of broad and specific tags related to the product and your niche.
- Thumbnails: Create eye-catching thumbnails that attract clicks. Use high-quality images, bold text, and visual elements that represent the product and review content.
- Closed Captions: Add closed captions or subtitles to make your video accessible to a wider audience. This also improves SEO, as YouTube can index the captions for search purposes.

6. Promoting Your Review

Promotion is essential to reach a larger audience and drive traffic to your review. Utilize various channels to maximize exposure.

- Social Media: Share your review on social media platforms like Facebook, Twitter, Instagram, and LinkedIn. Use relevant hashtags and engage with your followers to increase visibility.
- Community Engagement: Post your review in relevant online communities, forums, and groups. For example, share tech reviews in technology forums or beauty reviews in makeup enthusiast groups.

- Collaborations: Collaborate with other YouTubers or influencers in your niche. Guest appearances, shout-outs, or joint reviews can introduce your channel to a new audience.
- Email Marketing: If you have an email list, send out a newsletter featuring your latest review. Encourage subscribers to watch the video and share their feedback.

7. Monitoring and Analyzing Performance

Track the performance of your review to understand what works and what doesn't. Use this data to refine your future reviews and strategies.

- YouTube Analytics: Monitor key metrics such as views, watch time, engagement, and click-through rates on your affiliate links. Analyze which segments of the review performed best.
- Affiliate Analytics: Use affiliate marketing platforms to track clicks, conversions, and earnings from your links. Identify which products and strategies generate the most revenue.
- Feedback: Pay attention to viewer comments and feedback. Use this input to improve your content and address any questions or concerns.

8. Building Trust and Credibility

Building trust with your audience is crucial for successful affiliate marketing. Here are some ways to establish credibility:

- **Honesty:** Always provide honest and unbiased reviews. If you don't like a product, explain why. Transparency builds trust and keeps viewers coming back.
- **Disclosure:** Clearly disclose your affiliate relationships. This not only complies with legal requirements but also maintains your integrity.
- **Expertise:** Position yourself as an expert in your niche. Share your knowledge and experience, and continuously educate yourself about the latest trends and products.
- **Consistency:** Consistently produce high-quality reviews. Regular uploads help build a loyal audience and establish your channel as a reliable source of information.

9. Advanced Strategies for Maximizing Revenue

Once you have the basics down, consider implementing advanced strategies to further boost your affiliate marketing revenue.

- **Exclusive Offers:** Partner with brands to offer exclusive discounts or deals to your viewers. This creates a sense of urgency and incentivizes purchases.
- **Product Comparisons:** Create comparison videos between popular products in your niche. Highlight the differences and help viewers choose the best option for their needs.
- **Listicles:** Produce listicle videos, such as "Top 10 Smartphones of 2024," featuring multiple products with affiliate links. This format can attract more views and clicks.
- **Evergreen Content:** Focus on creating evergreen content that remains relevant over time. This ensures a steady stream of traffic and affiliate sales long after the initial upload.
- **Multiple Platforms:** Diversify your content across multiple platforms, such as blogs, podcasts, and social media, to reach a wider audience and increase affiliate link exposure.

10. Case Studies and Examples

To illustrate these strategies, let's look at a few successful YouTube channels that excel in affiliate marketing through engaging reviews:

- **MKBHD (Marques Brownlee):** Known for his high-quality tech reviews, Marques combines in-depth analysis, sleek production, and honest opinions. His credibility and expertise attract a large audience, leading to significant affiliate sales.

- Tati Westbrook: A beauty influencer who provides detailed makeup and skincare reviews. Tati's thorough evaluations, honesty, and engaging personality have built a loyal following and strong affiliate marketing revenue.
- Linus Tech Tips: A tech channel that offers a mix of product reviews, comparisons, and tutorials. Linus's team produces comprehensive and entertaining content, making their affiliate links highly effective.

Conclusion

Creating engaging reviews is an art that requires a deep understanding of your audience, thorough preparation, high-quality content creation, and strategic promotion. By following the steps outlined in this guide, you can effectively monetize your YouTube channel through affiliate marketing while building a loyal and engaged audience.

Remember, the key to success lies in authenticity, transparency, and continuous improvement. Stay true to your values, consistently deliver value to your viewers, and refine your strategies based on performance data and feedback. With dedication and effort, you can transform your YouTube channel into a powerful platform for affiliate marketing success.

CHAPTER NO. 2

Incorporating Tutorials: Leveraging Step-by-Step Guides for Effective Affiliate Marketing

Offering step-by-step tutorials or demonstrations showcasing how products can solve common problems is an excellent strategy to drive affiliate sales and provide valuable content to your audience. Tutorials not only educate viewers but also build trust and demonstrate the practical benefits of the products you are promoting. This comprehensive guide will cover the importance of tutorials, how to create effective tutorials, strategies for incorporating affiliate links, and best practices to maximize engagement and conversions.

1. The Importance of Tutorials in Affiliate Marketing

Tutorials are a powerful tool in affiliate marketing for several reasons:

- **Education:** They educate your audience on how to use a product effectively, showcasing its features and benefits.
- **Trust Building:** Providing valuable information helps establish you as an authority in your niche, building trust with your audience.
- **Problem Solving:** Demonstrating how a product solves common problems makes it more appealing and relevant to potential buyers.
- **Engagement:** Tutorials tend to be highly engaging, as viewers are actively seeking solutions to their problems.
- **Conversions:** A well-executed tutorial can significantly increase conversions by showing viewers exactly how a product works and why they need it.

2. Planning Your Tutorial

Effective tutorials require careful planning to ensure they meet the needs of your audience and align with your affiliate marketing goals.

- **Identify Common Problems:** Start by identifying common problems or pain points your audience faces. Use surveys, social media, and comments to gather insights.
- **Choose Relevant Products:** Select products that directly address the identified problems. Ensure the products are of high quality and have a positive reputation.
- **Research and Outline:** Research the product thoroughly and outline the steps of your tutorial. Make sure you cover all necessary details and anticipate any questions viewers might have.
- **Set Goals:** Define clear goals for your tutorial, such as educating your audience, increasing affiliate sales, or boosting engagement.

Example of Planning a Tutorial:
1. **Identify Problem:** Many viewers struggle with maintaining a home garden.
2. **Choose Product:** Select a high-quality gardening tool set that simplifies gardening tasks.
3. **Research and Outline:** Research the tool set and outline a step-by-step guide on how to use each tool effectively.
4. **Set Goals:** Aim to educate viewers on gardening techniques and drive affiliate sales for the tool set.

3. Creating Effective Tutorials

Creating engaging and informative tutorials involves several key steps:

- **Introduction:** Start with a brief introduction that explains the problem and introduces the product. Highlight the benefits of the product and why viewers should watch the tutorial.
- **Step-by-Step Instructions:** Provide clear, concise, and detailed step-by-step instructions. Use a logical sequence and ensure each step is easy to follow.
- **Visual Aids:** Use high-quality visuals, such as images, videos, and animations, to enhance understanding. Visual aids are especially important for complex tasks.
- **Practical Demonstrations:** Demonstrate the product in action, showing how it solves the problem. Use real-life scenarios to make the tutorial relatable.
- **Tips and Tricks:** Share additional tips and tricks to enhance the effectiveness of the product. This adds extra value to the tutorial.
- **Conclusion:** Summarize the key points, reiterate the benefits of the product, and include a clear call-to-action (CTA) encouraging viewers to click on your affiliate links.

Example of an Effective Tutorial Structure:
1. **Introduction:** "Welcome to our channel! Today, we're tackling common gardening challenges with the [Gardening Tool

Set]. This set makes gardening easier and more enjoyable. Let's dive in and see how it works."

2. **Step-by-Step Instructions:**
   - Step 1: "First, we'll use the trowel to prepare the soil. Make sure to loosen it up thoroughly."
   - Step 2: "Next, we'll plant the seeds using the planting tool. Ensure they're evenly spaced."
   - Step 3: "Use the weeder to remove any unwanted plants. This tool is great for precision."

3. **Visual Aids:** Include close-up shots of each tool in use, highlighting key features.

4. **Practical Demonstrations:** Show the entire process in a real garden, demonstrating the before-and-after effects.

5. **Tips and Tricks:** "A handy tip: Use the pruner to trim dead leaves regularly. This promotes healthy growth."

6. **Conclusion:** "There you have it! With the [Gardening Tool Set], gardening is a breeze. Click the link in the description to get your own set and start enjoying your garden more."

4. Incorporating Affiliate Links

Including affiliate links in your tutorials should be done thoughtfully and seamlessly to ensure they enhance the viewer's experience and drive conversions.

- **Description Links:** Include affiliate links in the video description. Place them near the top, so they're easily accessible. Provide a brief description and a compelling reason to click the link.
- **On-Screen Prompts:** Mention the affiliate links during the tutorial and use on-screen prompts to direct viewers to the description. For example, "Click the link below to get this tool set with a special discount."
- **Pinned Comments:** Pin a comment with your affiliate links to the top of the comment section. This ensures it remains visible to viewers who read comments.
- **Cards and End Screens:** Use YouTube's cards and end screens to add clickable links to your tutorial. These can direct viewers to related videos, playlists, or external sites where they can purchase the product.
- **Disclosure:** Always disclose your affiliate relationship to maintain transparency and trust with your audience. Use clear and straightforward language, such as "This video contains affiliate links. If you make a purchase through these links, we may earn a small commission at no extra cost to you."

Example of Incorporating Affiliate Links:
1. **Description Link:** "Get the [Gardening Tool Set] here: [Affiliate Link]. This set includes all the essential tools you need for a beautiful garden."

2. **On-Screen Prompt:** During the video, add a text overlay: "Special discount available in the description!"
3. **Pinned Comment:** "Loved the tutorial? Get your [Gardening Tool Set] here: [Affiliate Link]."
4. **Cards and End Screens:** Add a card at the end of the tutorial: "Want more gardening tips? Watch our next video!" and include an end screen with a link to the product.
5. **Disclosure:** Include a line in the description: "This video contains affiliate links. We may earn a commission if you make a purchase through these links."

5. Promoting Your Tutorial

Promotion is key to ensuring your tutorial reaches a wide audience and drives significant traffic to your affiliate links.

- **Social Media:** Share your tutorial on social media platforms such as Facebook, Twitter, Instagram, and LinkedIn. Use engaging captions and relevant hashtags to increase visibility.
- **Email Marketing:** Send the tutorial to your email subscribers, highlighting the benefits of the product and including a link to the video.
- **Blog Posts:** Write a blog post that complements your tutorial. Embed the video in the post and include affiliate links within the content.

- **Collaborations:** Collaborate with other influencers or YouTubers in your niche to cross-promote your tutorial. This can help you reach a broader audience.
- **SEO Optimization:** Optimize your video title, description, and tags with relevant keywords to improve searchability on YouTube and Google. This increases the chances of attracting organic traffic.

Example of Promoting Your Tutorial:
1. **Social Media:** "Struggling with gardening? Check out our latest tutorial on using the [Gardening Tool Set] to simplify your gardening tasks. Watch now and get a special discount: [Link] #gardening tips #homegarden"
2. **Email Marketing:** "Hi [Subscriber], we've just uploaded a new tutorial that's perfect for gardening enthusiasts like you. Learn how to use the [Gardening Tool Set] and enjoy a beautiful garden all year round. Watch now: [Link]"
3. **Blog Post:** Write a detailed blog post titled "Essential Gardening Tools for Beginners" and embed the tutorial video. Include affiliate links within the content.
4. **Collaborations:** Partner with a popular gardening blogger for a guest post or joint video.
5. **SEO Optimization:** Use keywords like "gardening tool set review," "how to use gardening tools," and "best gardening tools for beginners" in your video title, description, and tags.

6. Analyzing and Improving Your Tutorials

Regularly analyzing the performance of your tutorials helps you understand what works and what doesn't, allowing you to make necessary improvements.

- **YouTube Analytics:** Monitor key metrics such as views, watch time, engagement (likes, comments, shares), and click-through rates on your affiliate links. Identify which tutorials perform best and why.
- **Audience Feedback:** Pay attention to viewer comments and feedback. Use this input to improve your tutorials and address any common questions or concerns.
- **A/B Testing:** Experiment with different formats, styles, and CTAs to see what resonates most with your audience. For example, test different video lengths, presentation styles, or types of visual aids.
- **Affiliate Performance:** Track the performance of your affiliate links through your affiliate platform. Monitor clicks, conversions, and revenue generated from each link.

Example of Analyzing and Improving Your Tutorials:
1. **YouTube Analytics:** Check which tutorial has the highest engagement and affiliate link clicks. Analyze what made it successful and apply similar strategies to other tutorials.

2. **Audience Feedback:** Review comments for suggestions and common questions. Create follow-up tutorials or updates based on this feedback.
3. **A/B Testing:** Test two versions of a tutorial with different CTAs to see which one drives more conversions.
4. **Affiliate Performance:** Track the performance of your affiliate links to identify which products are most popular and why

CHAPTER NO. 3

Feature Product Comparisons: A Comprehensive Guide for YouTube Affiliate Marketing

Introduction

Product comparison videos are a powerful tool in the realm of YouTube affiliate marketing. By comparing various products within your niche and highlighting their pros and cons, you help viewers make informed decisions while simultaneously promoting affiliate products. This guide provides a comprehensive overview of how to create effective product comparison videos, with detailed strategies, tips, and examples to maximize your success.

---

1. Understanding the Importance of Product Comparison Videos

Why Product Comparison Videos?

1. **Informed Decision-Making:** Consumers often seek comparative information to understand which product best suits their needs.
2. **Trust Building:** Honest and transparent comparisons build trust with your audience, making them more likely to click on your affiliate links.
3. **Increased Engagement:** Comparison videos tend to attract more engagement due to their informative nature and the detailed analysis they provide.

4. **SEO Benefits:** These videos can rank well in search results, especially if they target long-tail keywords related to specific product comparisons.

Types of Products Suitable for Comparison

- **Technology:** Gadgets, software, cameras, smartphones, laptops, etc.
- **Beauty:** Skincare products, makeup brands, hair care tools, etc.
- **Fitness:** Workout equipment, fitness trackers, supplements, etc.
- **Home Decor:** Furniture, lighting, home appliances, etc.
- **Travel:** Luggage, travel accessories, accommodation options, etc.
- **Finance:** Credit cards, investment platforms, financial apps, etc.

---

2. Planning Your Product Comparison Video

Selecting Products to Compare

1. **Relevance:** Choose products that are relevant to your audience's interests and needs.
2. **Popularity:** Compare popular products that are frequently searched for and have a high potential for affiliate earnings.
3. **Variability:** Select products that have noticeable differences in features, pricing, or quality to provide a meaningful comparison.

Research and Preparation

1. **Gather Information:** Collect detailed information about each product's features, specifications, pricing, and user reviews.
2. **Use the Products:** If possible, use the products yourself to provide first-hand insights and authentic reviews.
3. **Create a Comparison Framework:** Outline the criteria you will use to compare the products, such as price, features, performance, ease of use, and customer support.

Creating a Script or Outline

1. **Introduction:** Briefly introduce the products you will be comparing and explain the purpose of the video.
2. **Product Overviews:** Provide a short overview of each product, including its key features and benefits.

3. **Detailed Comparison:** Compare the products based on the criteria outlined in your framework.
4. **Pros and Cons:** Highlight the strengths and weaknesses of each product.
5. **Conclusion and Recommendations:** Summarize your findings and provide recommendations based on different user needs.

---

3. Creating and Filming Your Product Comparison Video

Setting Up

1. **Lighting:** Ensure good lighting to clearly show the products and any details you discuss.
2. **Camera Setup:** Use a high-quality camera to capture clear and detailed footage.
3. **Background:** Choose a clean and neutral background to keep the focus on the products.

Filming Techniques

1. **Close-Ups:** Use close-up shots to highlight specific features of each product.
2. **Side-by-Side Comparisons:** Show the products side by side to visually compare their sizes, designs, and other physical attributes.
3. **Demonstrations:** Demonstrate the use of each product to show its functionality and ease of use.
4. **B-Roll Footage:** Include B-roll footage of the products being used in real-life scenarios.

Presenting the Information

1. **Be Objective:** Provide an unbiased comparison based on factual information.
2. **Use Visual Aids:** Incorporate charts, graphs, and text overlays to illustrate key points and comparisons.
3. **Engage with Viewers:** Encourage viewers to leave comments and ask questions about the products.

Editing Your Video

1. **Clear Structure:** Edit your video to ensure a logical flow from introduction to conclusion.
2. **Visual Enhancements:** Add text overlays, transitions, and effects to enhance the visual appeal.

3. **Audio Quality:** Ensure clear audio quality and consider adding background music to keep viewers engaged.
4. **CTA Placement:** Include clear call-to-actions (CTAs) throughout the video, especially at the end, to prompt viewers to click on your affiliate links.

---

4. Effective CTAs for Product Comparison Videos

Crafting Compelling CTAs

1. **Be Direct:** Use clear and concise language to instruct viewers on what action to take.
2. **Highlight Benefits:** Emphasize the benefits of clicking on the affiliate links, such as discounts or exclusive offers.
3. **Create Urgency:** Use phrases like "limited time offer" or "exclusive deal" to create a sense of urgency.

Examples of Effective CTAs

1. **Tech Comparison:** "Interested in getting one of these gadgets? Click the links in the description to find the best deals!"

2. **Beauty Comparison:** "Want to try these skincare products? Check out the links below to shop with exclusive discounts!"
3. **Fitness Comparison:** "Looking for the perfect fitness tracker? Click the links in the description to see more details and get a special offer!"

Placement Strategies

1. **In-Video Banners:** Use YouTube's in-video banners to display CTAs during key moments in your video.
2. **Video Descriptions:** Place affiliate links with clear CTAs at the top of your video descriptions.
3. **End Screens:** Utilize YouTube's end screens to direct viewers to your affiliate links as they finish watching your video.

---

5. Promoting Your Product Comparison Video

Optimizing for SEO

1. **Keyword Research:** Identify relevant keywords and phrases that your target audience is searching for.
2. **Title and Description:** Include your primary keywords in the video title and description to improve search visibility.
3. **Tags:** Use relevant tags to categorize your video and increase discoverability.

Sharing on Social Media

1. **Social Platforms:** Share your video on social media platforms like Facebook, Twitter, Instagram, and LinkedIn to reach a wider audience.
2. **Engagement:** Encourage your social media followers to watch, like, comment, and share your video.
3. **Teasers and Snippets:** Post short clips or teasers from your video to generate interest and drive traffic to your YouTube channel.

Collaborating with Influencers

1. **Partnerships:** Collaborate with other influencers in your niche to cross-promote each other's content.

2. **Guest Appearances:** Feature guest appearances in your videos or participate in joint comparison videos for added credibility.
3. **Shoutouts:** Give shoutouts to other influencers who share similar interests to build community and reach new audiences.

Engaging with Your Audience

1. **Respond to Comments:** Engage with viewers by responding to their comments and questions about the products.
2. **Polls and Surveys:** Conduct polls or surveys to understand your audience's preferences and tailor your content accordingly.
3. **Live Q&A Sessions:** Host live Q&A sessions to discuss the products in more detail and answer viewer queries in real-time.

---

6. Analyzing and Optimizing Your Performance

Tracking Metrics

1. **View Count:** Monitor the number of views your comparison video receives to gauge its reach.
2. **Engagement Rate:** Track likes, comments, shares, and other engagement metrics to assess viewer interaction.
3. **Click-Through Rate (CTR):** Measure the CTR of your affiliate links to understand how effectively your CTAs are driving clicks.
4. **Conversion Rate:** Analyze the conversion rate of your affiliate links to determine the effectiveness of your comparison video in driving sales.

Optimizing for Better Results

1. **A/B Testing:** Experiment with different CTAs, video formats, and presentation styles to see what resonates best with your audience.
2. **Feedback Loop:** Solicit feedback from your viewers to understand their preferences and improve your future videos.
3. **Continuous Improvement:** Use insights from your performance analysis to refine your content strategy and create more impactful comparison videos.

---

7. Examples of Successful Product Comparison Videos

Tech Comparison: Smartphones

Title: "iPhone 12 vs Samsung Galaxy S21: Which is Better for You?"
Content Overview:
- Introduction to both smartphones
- Detailed comparison of features, performance, and pricing
- Pros and cons of each device
- Conclusion and recommendations based on user needs
CTA Example: "Thinking of upgrading your smartphone? Check out the links in the description for the best deals on both models!"

Beauty Comparison: Skincare Products

Title: "Best Moisturizers for Dry Skin: CeraVe vs Neutrogena"
Content Overview:
- Overview of both moisturizers and their key ingredients
- Comparison of texture, effectiveness, and price
- Pros and cons of each product
- Conclusion and recommendations based on skin types

CTA Example: "Want to try these moisturizers? Click the links below to shop now and get a discount!"

Fitness Comparison: Fitness Trackers

Title: "Fitbit Charge 4 vs Garmin Vivosmart 4: Which One Should You Buy?"
Content Overview:
- Introduction to both fitness trackers
- Detailed comparison of features, accuracy, and battery life
- Pros and cons of each tracker
- Conclusion and recommendations based on fitness goals
CTA Example: "Looking for a new fitness tracker? Find the best deals in the description links!"

Conclusion

Product comparison videos are a highly effective strategy for YouTube affiliate marketing. By providing detailed and honest comparisons

CHAPTER NO. 4

Promoting special offers through affiliate marketing on YouTube can be highly effective across various niches. Here's an in-depth look at different niches, detailing how to share exclusive discounts and limited-time offers, creating urgency for viewers to buy:

1. **Technology and Gadgets**

Overview
The tech niche is one of the most lucrative and rapidly evolving sectors. It includes smartphones, laptops, cameras, smart home devices, software, and other gadgets.

Strategies for Promoting Special Offers
- **Product Reviews and Unboxings:** Showcase new gadgets and software with comprehensive reviews. Highlight exclusive discounts for early adopters.
- **Comparison Videos:** Compare different brands or models, and offer discount codes for the featured products.
- **Tutorials and How-Tos:** Create guides on setting up and using tech products, embedding affiliate links with special offers.
- **Limited-Time Deals:** Emphasize time-sensitive deals during product launches or special sales events like Black Friday or Cyber Monday.

Example
"Get 20% off the latest XYZ smartphone when you use my affiliate link below! Hurry, this offer is valid only for the next 48 hours!"

2. **Beauty and Skincare**

Overview
The beauty and skincare industry is vast, encompassing makeup, skincare routines, hair care products, and wellness treatments.

Strategies for Promoting Special Offers
- **Makeup Tutorials:** Share makeup routines featuring affiliate-linked products with exclusive discount codes.
- **Skincare Regimens:** Discuss daily skincare routines and offer special discounts on featured products.
- **Product Hauls:** Show off recent purchases and collaborations with beauty brands, offering viewers a chance to buy at discounted rates.
- **Seasonal Promotions:** Promote discounts tied to seasons or holidays, like summer skincare essentials or holiday makeup looks.

Example
"Use the code BEAUTY20 at checkout for a 20% discount on all skincare products from ABC brand, valid until the end of the month!"

3. **Health and Fitness**

Overview

This niche covers fitness equipment, supplements, workout programs, and health-related products.

Strategies for Promoting Special Offers
- **Workout Routines:** Share workout videos featuring equipment or supplements, with discount codes for viewers.
- **Healthy Recipes:** Provide healthy meal prep ideas using affiliate-linked ingredients or cookware.
- **Fitness Challenges:** Launch fitness challenges and offer exclusive discounts on related products.
- **Supplement Reviews:** Review health supplements and provide special offers for first-time buyers.

Example
"Join my 30-day fitness challenge and get 15% off on all XYZ brand supplements with the code FIT15!"

4. **Fashion and Apparel**

Overview
Fashion and apparel include clothing, accessories, shoes, and jewelry. It's a highly visual niche, perfect for YouTube.

Strategies for Promoting Special Offers

- **Lookbooks:** Create seasonal lookbooks with links to discounted items.
- **Try-On Hauls:** Show clothing hauls from affiliate partners, sharing discount codes with viewers.
- **Styling Tips:** Offer styling advice and exclusive offers on featured pieces.
- **Holiday Promotions:** Promote special holiday sales, like back-to-school, Black Friday, or holiday gift guides.

Example
"Get 25% off your first purchase at XYZ fashion brand with the code STYLE25! This offer is valid only for this week!"

5. **Home and Garden**

Overview
This niche covers home improvement, gardening, décor, furniture, and DIY projects.

Strategies for Promoting Special Offers
- **DIY Projects:** Share DIY home improvement or gardening projects, with discounts on the materials or tools used.
- **Home Tours:** Showcase different home décor styles and offer discounts on featured furniture or décor items.

- **Gardening Tips:** Provide gardening tips and tricks, promoting special offers on tools and plants.
- **Seasonal Decor:** Highlight seasonal decoration ideas with exclusive discounts on featured items.

Example
"Transform your garden with 20% off on all gardening tools from XYZ brand using the code GARDEN20, valid for a limited time only!"

6. **Travel and Adventure**

Overview
The travel niche includes travel gear, booking services, travel guides, and adventure activities.

Strategies for Promoting Special Offers
- **Travel Vlogs:** Document travel experiences and offer discounts on travel gear or booking services.
- **Packing Tips:** Share packing tips and provide special offers on luggage and travel accessories.
- **Destination Guides:** Create guides to different travel destinations, promoting discounts on tours or hotels.

- **Adventure Activities:** Highlight adventure activities like hiking or scuba diving, with exclusive discounts on related gear or experiences.

Example
"Book your next adventure with a 10% discount on XYZ travel gear using the code TRAVEL10! Offer valid for a limited time."

7. **Food and Cooking**

Overview
This niche encompasses cooking equipment, ingredients, meal kits, and gourmet products.

Strategies for Promoting Special Offers
- **Recipe Videos:** Share recipes and offer discounts on ingredients or cooking tools.
- **Cooking Classes:** Promote online cooking classes with special discounts for your viewers.
- **Product Reviews:** Review gourmet products or kitchen gadgets, providing exclusive discount codes.
- **Meal Prep:** Offer meal prep ideas and discounts on meal kit services.

Example

"Get 15% off your first order of gourmet spices from XYZ brand with the code COOK15, valid until the end of the month!"

8. **Finance and Investments**

Overview
This niche covers personal finance, investing, budgeting, and financial tools.

Strategies for Promoting Special Offers
- **Budgeting Tips:** Share budgeting tips and promote special offers on financial tools or apps.
- **Investment Strategies:** Discuss investment strategies and provide exclusive discounts on related courses or software.
- **Financial Reviews:** Review financial products or services, offering discount codes for sign-ups.
- **Saving Hacks:** Offer saving hacks and promote discounts on money-saving products or services.

Example
"Sign up for the XYZ investment app and get a 20% discount on your first year's subscription with the code INVEST20, valid for a limited time!"

9. **Education and Self-Improvement**

Overview
This niche includes online courses, self-help books, productivity tools, and personal development programs.

Strategies for Promoting Special Offers
- **Course Reviews:** Review online courses and provide exclusive discount codes for enrolment.
- **Productivity Tips:** Share productivity tips and promote special offers on tools or software.
- **Book Recommendations:** Recommend self-help books with discount links for purchases.
- **Self-Improvement Challenges:** Launch self-improvement challenges and offer discounts on related products or services.

Example
"Unlock your potential with 20% off XYZ online course using the code LEARN20, valid until the end of the month!"

10. **Gaming and Entertainment**

Overview

This niche covers video games, gaming accessories, entertainment systems, and streaming services.

Strategies for Promoting Special Offers
- **Gameplay Reviews:** Review video games and provide discount codes for purchases.
- **Gaming Setups:** Showcase gaming setups and offer exclusive discounts on gaming accessories.
- **Streaming Recommendations:** Recommend streaming services and share special offers for subscriptions.
- **Limited-Edition Releases:** Promote limited-edition game releases or merchandise with exclusive discounts.

Example
"Get 15% off on all gaming accessories from XYZ brand with the code GAME15, valid for a limited time only!"

Conclusion

Promoting special offers through affiliate marketing on YouTube requires a strategic approach tailored to your niche. By sharing exclusive discounts and limited-time offers, you can create a sense of urgency that encourages viewers to make purchases. Whether you're in technology, beauty, health, fashion, home and garden, travel, food, finance, education, or gaming, these strategies can help you effectively leverage affiliate marketing to boost your income.

Remember to stay authentic and transparent with your audience, providing genuine recommendations that add value to their lives. With the right approach, you can build trust and a loyal following, ensuring long-term success in your affiliate marketing efforts.

CHAPTER NO. 5

Using Call-to-Actions (CTAs) to Boost Affiliate Link Clicks on YouTube

Introduction

Call-to-Actions (CTAs) are an integral part of any marketing strategy, particularly in affiliate marketing on YouTube. A well-crafted CTA guides your audience towards a specific action, such as clicking on affiliate links, subscribing to your channel, or purchasing a product. This comprehensive guide will delve into the importance of CTAs, how to create effective ones, and detailed strategies for various niches to maximize your affiliate marketing success.

---

1. Understanding Call-to-Actions (CTAs)

What is a CTA?

A Call-to-Action (CTA) is a prompt that encourages your audience to take a specific action. In the context of YouTube affiliate marketing, a CTA typically directs viewers to click on an affiliate link provided in the video description, pinned comment, or on-screen overlay.

Why are CTAs Important?

CTAs are crucial because they:
- **Drive Conversions:** A clear and compelling CTA can significantly increase the likelihood of viewers clicking on your affiliate links.

- **Guide Audience Behavior:** CTAs help direct your audience towards desired actions, enhancing the overall effectiveness of your marketing strategy.
- **Enhance Engagement:** Encouraging viewers to interact with your content through CTAs can boost engagement metrics such as likes, comments, and shares.

---

2. Elements of an Effective CTA

Clarity

Your CTA should be clear and direct. Viewers need to understand exactly what action you want them to take and why. Avoid vague language and be specific about the desired action.

Example:
- Instead of saying, "Check out the description," say, "Click the link in the description to buy this product at a 20% discount!"

Relevance

Ensure that your CTA is relevant to the content of your video and resonates with your audience's interests. A CTA that aligns with the viewer's needs and the video's context will be more effective.

Example:
- In a tech review video, a relevant CTA could be, "Get the latest tech gadgets with my special discount link below!"

Urgency

Creating a sense of urgency can motivate viewers to act quickly. Phrases like "limited time offer," "exclusive discount," or "while supplies last" can spur immediate action.

Example:
- "Hurry, this offer ends soon! Click the link in the description to get 50% off!"

Value Proposition

Highlight the benefit of taking the action. What will the viewer gain by clicking your affiliate link? Emphasize the value they will receive, whether it's a discount, bonus content, or useful resources.

Example:
- "Download this free eBook using the link in the description to learn more about effective marketing strategies."

---

3. Crafting Your CTAs

Step-by-Step Guide

1. **Identify the Desired Action:**
   Determine the specific action you want your viewers to take, such as clicking an affiliate link, subscribing to your channel, or signing up for a newsletter.

2. **Use Direct Language:**
   Be clear and concise in your wording. Use action verbs like "click," "buy," "subscribe," and "download."

3. **Incorporate Benefits:**
   Highlight what the viewer will gain by taking the action. Emphasize the value or benefits they will receive.

4. **Create Urgency:**
   If applicable, use time-sensitive language to encourage immediate action. Phrases like "limited time," "exclusive," and "act now" can be effective.

5. **Align with Video Content:**
   Ensure your CTA is relevant to the content of the video and flows naturally within the narrative.

Examples of Effective CTAs

1. **Tech Review Video:**
   "Love this gadget? Click the link in the description to buy it now and get 10% off with my special discount code!"

2. **Beauty Tutorial:**
   "Want to recreate this look? All the products I used are linked in the description. Click here to shop!"

3. **Fitness Routine:**
   "Get the gear I'm using in this workout. Click the link in the description for a special offer on all items!"

4. **Travel Vlog:**

"Planning a trip here? Check out my recommended travel gear in the links below for exclusive discounts!"

---

4. Placing Your CTAs

In-Video CTAs

In-video CTAs are prompts that appear directly within your video content. They can be verbal, visual, or both. Here's how to effectively place them:

1. **Verbal Prompts:**
   Mention your CTA during key moments in the video. For instance, if you're reviewing a product, verbally prompt viewers to check the description for a purchase link.

2. **On-Screen Text:**
   Display text overlays with your CTA. Ensure the text is clear and contrasts well with the video background for easy readability.

3. **Annotations and Cards:**

Use YouTube's annotation and cards features to add clickable links within your video. These can direct viewers to external websites or additional content.

Video Descriptions

The video description is a prime location for your affiliate links and CTAs. Here's how to optimize it:

1. **Top of the Description:**
   Place your primary CTA and affiliate link at the very beginning of the description to ensure visibility.

2. **Detailed Information:**
   Provide a brief explanation of the product or offer and why viewers should click the link. This additional context can encourage clicks.

3. **Consistent Format:**
   Use a consistent format for your descriptions across all videos. This helps regular viewers know where to find the information they're looking for.

Pinned Comments

Pinned comments appear at the top of the comment section, making them highly visible. Here's how to use them effectively:

1. **Pin Your Comment:**
   Post a comment with your CTA and affiliate link, then pin it to the top of the comment section.

2. **Engage with Viewers:**
   Encourage viewers to interact with the pinned comment by asking questions or prompting discussions related to the video content.

End Screens and Cards

End screens and cards are YouTube features that allow you to promote other videos, playlists, or external links. Here's how to use them:

1. **End Screens:**
   At the end of your video, use end screens to direct viewers to related content or your affiliate link. Ensure it aligns with the video content they just watched.

2. **Cards:**

Insert cards at relevant points in your video to promote your affiliate link. Cards can appear as a small, clickable icon in the upper right corner of the video.

---

5. Niche-Specific CTA Strategies

Different niches require tailored CTAs to effectively engage viewers and encourage clicks. Here are detailed strategies for various popular niches:

1. Technology (Tech)

Audience Insights
Tech enthusiasts are constantly on the lookout for the latest gadgets, software, and innovations. They value detailed reviews, unboxings, and tutorials that help them make informed decisions.

Effective CTAs for Tech
1. **Unboxing Videos:**
   "Check out the link in the description to get your hands on this latest gadget at a special price!"

2. **Tutorials:**
   "Want to try this software yourself? Click the link below for a free trial and exclusive discount."

3. **Reviews:**
   "If you're interested in purchasing this product, use my link to get an extra warranty and support my channel."

Placement Strategies
- **In-Video Banners:** Use YouTube's in-video banners to display CTAs during key moments in your video.
- **Video Descriptions:** Always include affiliate links with a clear CTA at the top of your video descriptions.
- **End Screens:** Utilize YouTube's end screens to direct viewers to your affiliate links as they finish watching your video.

2. Beauty

Audience Insights
Beauty aficionados look for honest product reviews, makeup tutorials, and skincare routines. They value personal recommendations and trust influencers who share their beauty journeys.

Effective CTAs for Beauty

1. **Makeup Tutorials:**
   "Love this look? Shop the products I used with the links below!"

2. **Product Reviews:**
   "This skincare product has transformed my routine. Click the link to see more details and get a discount."

3. **Hauls:**
   "Curious about these beauty buys? Find all the links in the description and use my code for a special offer."

Placement Strategies
- **Pinned Comments:** Pin a comment with your affiliate link and a CTA at the top of the comment section.
- **Instagram Integration:** Use Instagram stories and posts to direct followers to your YouTube video, where they can find affiliate links.
- **Mid-Roll CTAs:** Integrate CTAs naturally within your content, especially during product showcases.

3. Fitness

Audience Insights

Fitness enthusiasts seek workout routines, nutrition advice, and gear recommendations. They are motivated by results and appreciate practical tips from experienced fitness influencers.

Effective CTAs for Fitness
1. **Workout Routines:**
   "Try this workout routine with the gear I'm using. Links in the description!"

2. **Nutrition Advice:**
   "Want to supplement your diet? Click the link for my favorite protein powder and get a discount."

3. **Product Endorsements:**
   "These fitness trackers have improved my workouts. Check out the link to find the best one for you."

Placement Strategies
- **Interactive Cards:** Use YouTube's cards feature to insert affiliate links at relevant points in your videos.
- **Blog Integration:** Link your YouTube videos to your fitness blog where you can provide more detailed reviews and affiliate

CHAPTER NO. 6

Collaborate with Brands: Partnering for Sponsored Content with Affiliate Links

Introduction

Collaborating with brands for sponsored content is a strategic approach to enhance your affiliate marketing efforts on YouTube. Sponsored content allows you to build mutually beneficial relationships with brands, providing value to your audience while generating additional income. This comprehensive guide will cover the essentials of brand collaborations, including how to identify potential partners, negotiate deals, create engaging content, and measure success.

---

1. Understanding Brand Collaborations

What is a Brand Collaboration?

A brand collaboration involves partnering with a company to create content that promotes their products or services. In exchange, you receive compensation, which can be monetary or in the form of free products, exclusive discounts, or other perks. When combined with affiliate links, these collaborations can significantly boost your earnings.

Why Collaborate with Brands?

1. **Increased Revenue:** Sponsored content provides an additional income stream beyond traditional affiliate commissions.
2. **Enhanced Credibility:** Partnering with reputable brands can enhance your credibility and authority in your niche.
3. **Exclusive Offers:** Brands often provide exclusive discounts or offers that you can share with your audience, increasing the likelihood of conversions.
4. **Expanded Reach:** Collaborations can expose your channel to new audiences through cross-promotion with the brand.

---

2. Identifying Potential Brand Partners

Researching Brands

1. **Niche Relevance:** Identify brands that are relevant to your niche and audience interests. The products or services they offer should align with the content you create.
2. **Brand Reputation:** Partner with reputable brands that have positive reviews and a strong market presence. This ensures that the products you promote are of high quality.
3. **Audience Demand:** Choose brands that offer products or services that your audience is interested in or has expressed a need for.

Tools for Finding Brands

1. **Affiliate Networks:** Platforms like ShareASale, CJ Affiliate, and Rakuten Advertising list numerous brands looking for affiliates and influencers to collaborate with.
2. **Social Media:** Use social media platforms to discover brands that are actively engaging with influencers. Look for hashtags like #sponsored, #ad, or #brand collaboration.
3. **Industry Events:** Attend industry conferences, trade shows, and online webinars to network with potential brand partners.

Approaching Brands

1. **Professional Email:** Craft a professional and personalized email to introduce yourself and your channel. Highlight your audience demographics, engagement metrics, and how a collaboration would benefit the brand.
2. **Media Kit:** Create a media kit that includes your channel statistics, audience insights, previous collaboration examples, and testimonials. This provides brands with a comprehensive overview of your influence.
3. **Proposal:** Develop a detailed collaboration proposal outlining the type of content you plan to create, the integration of affiliate links, and the potential reach and impact.

---

3. Negotiating Collaboration Deals

Setting Terms and Conditions

1. **Compensation:** Negotiate a fair compensation package, which can include a flat fee, commission on sales, or a combination of both. Ensure that the compensation reflects the value you bring to the collaboration.

2. **Content Requirements:** Clarify the type and frequency of content you will create, such as videos, social media posts, or blog articles. Specify the inclusion of affiliate links and any brand messaging guidelines.
3. **Usage Rights:** Determine the usage rights for the content you create. Specify whether the brand can repurpose the content on their platforms and for how long.
4. **Exclusivity:** Discuss any exclusivity agreements, such as not promoting competing brands within a specified timeframe.

Contracts and Agreements

1. **Written Agreement:** Always have a written contract outlining the terms and conditions of the collaboration. This protects both parties and ensures clear expectations.
2. **Legal Review:** If possible, have a legal professional review the contract to ensure all aspects are fair and legally binding.
3. **Payment Terms:** Clearly outline the payment schedule, including any upfront payments, milestones, and final payments. Specify the payment method and any invoicing requirements.

---

4. Creating Engaging Sponsored Content

Aligning Content with Audience Interests

1. **Relevance:** Ensure that the sponsored content aligns with your audience's interests and adds value. Authentic and relevant content is more likely to resonate with viewers.
2. **Transparency:** Be transparent with your audience about sponsored content. Clearly disclose that the video is sponsored and include any necessary disclaimers as per platform guidelines.
3. **Integration:** Seamlessly integrate the brand and affiliate links into your content. Avoid making the content feel like a commercial; instead, weave the promotion naturally into your narrative.

Types of Sponsored Content

1. **Product Reviews:** Provide an in-depth review of the brand's product, highlighting its features, benefits, and your personal experience. Include affiliate links in the video description and mention them in the video.
2. **Tutorials and How-Tos:** Create tutorials or how-to videos demonstrating how to use the brand's product. This can be particularly effective for tech, beauty, and fitness niches.
3. **Unboxings:** Film unboxing videos to showcase the brand's product as you unpack it. Share your first impressions and direct viewers to affiliate links for more information.

4. **Hauls and Favorites:** Incorporate the brand's product into a haul or favorites video, where you feature multiple items. This provides context and shows how the product fits into your lifestyle.

Best Practices for Sponsored Content

1. **Authenticity:** Be genuine in your promotion. Share your honest opinions and experiences with the product, as authenticity builds trust with your audience.
2. **Engagement:** Encourage viewer engagement by asking questions, prompting comments, and responding to feedback. This interaction can increase the video's reach and impact.
3. **High-Quality Production:** Invest in high-quality production to make your content visually appealing and professional. Good lighting, clear audio, and crisp visuals enhance the viewer experience.
4. **Call-to-Action (CTA):** Include a strong call-to-action directing viewers to click on the affiliate links. Highlight any special offers or discounts provided by the brand.

---

5. Promoting Your Sponsored Content

Optimizing for Search Engines

1. **Keyword Research:** Identify relevant keywords that potential viewers are searching for. Use tools like Google Keyword Planner, Ahrefs, or SEMrush to find high-traffic keywords related to the product.
2. **Title and Description:** Include primary keywords in the video title and description to improve search visibility. Make sure the title is compelling and accurately represents the content.
3. **Tags:** Use relevant tags to categorize your video and increase discoverability on YouTube.

Sharing on Social Media

1. **Cross-Promotion:** Share your sponsored content across all your social media platforms, such as Facebook, Twitter, Instagram, and LinkedIn. Tailor your posts to each platform's audience and format.
2. **Engaging Posts:** Create engaging posts that tease the content and encourage followers to watch the full video. Use eye-catching visuals, intriguing captions, and relevant hashtags.
3. **Stories and Reels:** Utilize Instagram Stories, Reels, and other short-form content formats to promote your sponsored video. These can drive traffic to your YouTube channel and affiliate links.

Email Marketing

1. **Newsletter:** Include the sponsored content in your email newsletter, highlighting the collaboration and providing a direct link to the video.
2. **Exclusive Offers:** If the brand provides exclusive discounts or offers, share these with your email subscribers to incentivize clicks on affiliate links.

Collaborating with Influencers

1. **Joint Campaigns:** Partner with other influencers in your niche for joint campaigns. This can expand your reach and introduce your content to new audiences.
2. **Shoutouts and Mentions:** Exchange shoutouts and mentions with other influencers to promote each other's sponsored content. This cross-promotion can boost visibility and engagement.

---

6. Measuring the Success of Your Collaboration

Key Metrics to Track

1. **Views and Watch Time:** Monitor the number of views and total watch time of your sponsored video to gauge its reach and viewer interest.
2. **Engagement Rate:** Track likes, comments, shares, and other engagement metrics to assess how well the content resonates with your audience.
3. **Click-Through Rate (CTR):** Measure the CTR of your affiliate links to determine how effectively your CTAs are driving clicks.
4. **Conversion Rate:** Analyze the conversion rate of your affiliate links to understand the effectiveness of the collaboration in driving sales.
5. **Revenue:** Calculate the total revenue generated from the collaboration, including any upfront payments, commissions, and bonuses.

Analyzing Performance

1. **Compare Metrics:** Compare the performance metrics of your sponsored content with other videos on your channel. Look for trends and patterns that can inform future collaborations.

2. **Audience Feedback:** Review comments and feedback from your audience to understand their perception of the sponsored content. Use this feedback to improve future collaborations.
3. **Brand Feedback:** Communicate with the brand to share performance insights and gather their feedback on the collaboration. This can help strengthen the partnership and improve future projects.

Optimizing Future Collaborations

1. **Refine Your Approach:** Use the insights gained from performance analysis to refine your approach to brand collaborations. Experiment with different content formats, CTAs, and promotional strategies.
2. **Build Long-Term Relationships:** Focus on building long-term relationships with brands that align well with your niche and audience. Consistent collaborations can provide stable income and reliable content opportunities.
3. **Expand Your Network:** Continuously seek out new brands to collaborate with, expanding your network and diversifying your revenue streams.

Conclusion

Collaborating with brands for sponsored content is a powerful strategy to enhance your affiliate marketing efforts on YouTube. By partnering with reputable brands, you can provide valuable content to your audience, build credibility,

CHAPTER NO. 7

Hosting Giveaways in YouTube Affiliate Marketing: A Comprehensive Guide

Introduction

Giveaways are a powerful strategy in YouTube affiliate marketing for engaging your audience, increasing brand awareness, and driving affiliate sales. By offering viewers a chance to win products linked to your affiliates, you create excitement, encourage participation, and ultimately boost your channel's growth and revenue. This guide explores everything you need to know about hosting giveaways on YouTube, from planning and executing to maximizing their effectiveness in your affiliate marketing strategy.

---

1. Understanding the Benefits of Hosting Giveaways

Engagement and Interaction

- **Increase Viewer Engagement:** Giveaways encourage viewers to interact with your content by liking, commenting, and sharing your videos.
- **Build Community:** They foster a sense of community among your audience, encouraging them to connect with each other and with your brand.
- **Boost Subscriber Count:** Giveaways often require participants to subscribe to your channel, helping to grow your subscriber base.

Brand Awareness and Exposure

- **Expand Reach:** Giveaways attract new viewers who may not have discovered your channel otherwise, expanding your audience reach.
- **Enhance Brand Visibility:** Associating your brand with popular or desirable products increases brand visibility and recognition.

Drive Affiliate Sales

- **Promote Affiliate Products:** Giveaways provide a platform to showcase affiliate-linked products, driving traffic and potential sales through affiliate links.
- **Increase Conversion Rates:** Viewers who engage in giveaways are more likely to explore and purchase products linked through your affiliate links.

SEO and Channel Growth

- **Improve SEO:** Increased engagement from giveaways can improve your video's ranking on YouTube, leading to higher visibility and organic growth.
- **Long-term Benefits:** A successful giveaway can lead to sustained growth in subscribers, views, and engagement even after the giveaway ends.

---

2. Planning Your Giveaway Strategy

Setting Objectives

- **Define Goals:** Determine what you aim to achieve with the giveaway—whether it's increasing subscribers, promoting a specific product, or boosting engagement metrics.

Choosing Giveaway Prizes

- **Relevance:** Select prizes that align with your channel's niche and audience interests to ensure maximum participation and relevance.
- **Quality:** Choose high-quality products that appeal to your audience and reflect positively on your brand and affiliates.

Determining Entry Requirements

- **Subscribe to Your Channel:** Require participants to subscribe to your YouTube channel to increase your subscriber base.

- **Engagement Actions:** Encourage actions such as liking the video, leaving a comment, sharing the video, or following your social media channels.

Legal Considerations

- **Disclosure:** Clearly disclose all giveaway terms, eligibility criteria, and rules to participants.
- **Compliance:** Ensure compliance with YouTube's policies and guidelines regarding giveaways and promotions.

Promotion Strategy

- **Teasers and Announcements:** Build anticipation by teasing the giveaway in advance and making announcements across your social media platforms.
- **Collaborations:** Partner with other influencers for brands to expand reach and increase giveaway visibility.

---

3. Executing Your Giveaway

Creating Giveaway Content

- **Video Announcement:** Create a dedicated video announcing the giveaway, explaining the rules, and showcasing the prizes.
- **Visual Appeal:** Use high-quality visuals and graphics to make the giveaway announcement visually appealing and engaging.

Promoting Your Giveaway

- **Video Description:** Include detailed giveaway instructions, rules, and links to affiliate products in the video description.
- **Social Media Promotion:** Share giveaway announcements and updates on your social media platforms to reach a broader audience.

Monitoring and Moderation

- **Moderate Entries:** Monitor and moderate entries to ensure compliance with giveaway rules and eligibility criteria.
- **Engage with Participants:** Respond to comments, answer questions, and engage with participants to build excitement and trust.

Choosing a Winner

- **Fair Selection Process:** Use a random selection tool or method to choose a winner transparently and fairly.
- **Announcement:** Announce the winner publicly and promptly to maintain transparency and credibility.

---

4. Maximizing Giveaway Effectiveness

Encouraging Participation

- **Clear Instructions:** Provide clear and simple instructions for participating in the giveaway to reduce barriers to entry.
- **Engaging Content:** Create compelling content that encourages viewers to participate by highlighting the benefits of entering.

Utilizing Affiliate Links

- **Prominent Placement:** Feature affiliate links prominently in the giveaway announcement video and description to drive traffic and potential sales.

- **Bonus Entries:** Offer bonus entries for participants who use affiliate links to purchase products or sign up for services.

Post-Giveaway Engagement

- **Follow-Up Content:** Create follow-up content such as winner announcements, product reviews, or unboxing videos to maintain engagement.
- **Feedback and Insights:** Gather feedback from participants to improve future giveaways and understand audience preferences.

---

5. Legal and Compliance Considerations

Giveaway Rules and Guidelines

- **Clear Terms and Conditions:** Clearly outline giveaway rules, eligibility criteria, entry deadlines, and prize details in the video description and official giveaway announcement.
- **Compliance:** Ensure compliance with local laws, YouTube's policies, and guidelines regarding giveaways, contests, and promotions.

Data Privacy

- **Participant Information:** Handle participant data responsibly and in accordance with data protection regulations (e.g., GDPR) to maintain trust and credibility.

Disclaimers and Disclosures

- **Affiliate Links:** Disclose all affiliate relationships and links in accordance with FTC guidelines to maintain transparency with your audience.
- **Not Endorsed by YouTube:** Clarify that the giveaway is not endorsed, sponsored, or administered by YouTube.

---

6. Analyzing Giveaway Performance

Measuring Success Metrics

- **Engagement Metrics:** Track metrics such as views, likes, comments, shares, and subscriber growth to gauge engagement levels.

- **Conversion Rates:** Analyze affiliate link clicks and conversions to assess the giveaway's impact on driving sales.

Feedback and Insights

- **Participant Feedback:** Solicit feedback from participants to gain insights into their preferences, experiences, and suggestions for improvement.
- **Performance Analysis:** Use data and feedback to evaluate the effectiveness of the giveaway and inform future giveaway strategies.

---

7. Examples of Successful Giveaways

Tech Products Giveaway

- **Prizes:** High-end headphones, gaming consoles, or smart home devices.
- **Entry Requirements:** Subscribe to the channel, like the video, comment on why they want to win, and share the giveaway announcement on social media.

- **Promotion:** Tease the giveaway in tech review videos and promote across social media channels.

Beauty Products Giveaway

- **Prizes:** Luxury skincare sets, makeup palettes, or beauty toolkits.
- **Entry Requirements:** Subscribe, like, comment with their favorite beauty tip, and share the giveaway on Instagram or Facebook.
- **Promotion:** Feature the giveaway in makeup tutorial videos and collaborate with beauty influencers for wider reach.

Fitness Gear Giveaway

- **Prizes:** Fitness trackers, home workout equipment, or sports apparel.
- **Entry Requirements:** Subscribe, like, comment on their fitness goals, and share the giveaway on Twitter or Pinterest.
- **Promotion:** Highlight the giveaway in fitness routine videos and partner with fitness influencers for cross-promotion.

Conclusion

Hosting giveaways on YouTube can be a highly effective strategy for engaging your audience, promoting affiliate products, and growing your channel. By carefully planning, executing, and analyzing your giveaways, you can maximize their impact, increase brand visibility, and drive affiliate sales. Remember to prioritize transparency, compliance with regulations, and ethical practices to build trust with your audience and ensure long-term success in your affiliate marketing efforts.

CHAPTER NO. 8

Creating Evergreen Content for YouTube Affiliate Marketing

Introduction

Evergreen content is the cornerstone of sustained success in YouTube affiliate marketing. Unlike trending or time-sensitive content, evergreen videos remain relevant and valuable to viewers over an extended period. This comprehensive guide explores the strategies, benefits, and practical tips for creating evergreen content that continues to attract views and generate affiliate income long after its initial upload.

---

1. Understanding Evergreen Content

What is Evergreen Content?

Evergreen content refers to videos that retain their relevance and value to audiences indefinitely. These videos are not tied to current events or trends but instead address timeless topics and provide enduring solutions or information.

Benefits of Evergreen Content

1. **Consistent Views:** Evergreen videos continue to attract views over time, often becoming a steady source of traffic for your channel.
2. **Long-Term SEO Benefits:** These videos can rank well in search engines, driving organic traffic months or even years after being published.
3. **Stable Affiliate Income:** By featuring evergreen topics related to affiliate products, you can generate consistent affiliate income as viewers discover and engage with your content.
4. **Builds Authority:** Creating valuable evergreen content establishes your expertise in your niche, enhancing your channel's credibility among viewers and potential affiliates.

Examples of Evergreen Content Ideas

- **How-to Guides:** Tutorials on using specific products or achieving certain outcomes.
- **Product Reviews:** In-depth reviews of popular products in your niche.
- **Top 10 Lists:** Compilations of best products, tools, or resources.
- **Educational Content:** Lessons, tips, or strategies relevant to your audience.
- **FAQs and Troubleshooting:** Answers to common questions or issues in your niche.

- **Historical Overviews:** Insights into the evolution or background of products or technologies.

---

2. Planning Evergreen Content Strategy

Identifying Evergreen Topics

1. **Keyword Research:** Use SEO tools to identify keywords and phrases with consistent search volume and low competition.
2. **Audience Needs:** Address common pain points or interests within your niche that are unlikely to change over time.
3. **Evergreen Formats:** Choose content formats (e.g., tutorials, reviews, guides) that lend themselves to timeless relevance and value.

Content Planning and Calendar

1. **Content Calendar:** Develop a schedule for producing and publishing evergreen content, ensuring consistency in your uploads.
2. **Topic Rotation:** Balance evergreen videos with other types of content to maintain audience interest and engagement.

3. **Update Strategy:** Plan periodic updates for evergreen videos to ensure information remains accurate and relevant.

Research and Preparation

1. **Thorough Research:** Gather comprehensive information and data related to your chosen evergreen topic.
2. **Script or Outline:** Create a detailed script or outline to structure your content logically and ensure key points are covered.
3. **Visuals and Examples:** Prepare visuals, demonstrations, or examples that enhance viewer understanding and engagement.

---

3. Creating Evergreen Content: Best Practices

Quality Production

1. **High-Quality Video and Audio:** Use professional equipment to ensure clear visuals and audio quality.
2. **Engaging Presentation:** Maintain a lively and engaging delivery to captivate viewers throughout the video.

3. **Visual Aids:** Incorporate graphics, charts, or demonstrations to illustrate key points effectively.

Content Structure

1. **Introduction:** Clearly introduce the topic and what viewers can expect to learn or gain from watching.
2. **Main Content:** Present information in a structured and logical manner, addressing the topic comprehensively.
3. **Conclusion:** Recap key points and provide a clear takeaway or call-to-action (CTA) for viewers.

SEO Optimization

1. **Keyword Integration:** Naturally include relevant keywords in your video title, description, and tags.
2. **Optimized Metadata:** Write compelling titles and descriptions that encourage clicks and accurately reflect the video content.
3. **Thumbnails:** Design eye-catching thumbnails that attract attention and accurately represent the video's content.

---

4. Promoting Evergreen Content

SEO and Organic Reach

1. **Optimize Titles and Descriptions:** Use compelling titles and detailed descriptions with relevant keywords.
2. **Build Backlinks:** Promote your videos on your website, blog, and social media platforms to increase backlinks and improve SEO.
3. **Collaborate and Guest Post:** Collaborate with influencers or guest posts on relevant platforms to expand your content's reach.

Email Marketing

1. **Newsletter Promotion:** Include links to your evergreen content in your email newsletters to drive traffic from your subscriber base.
2. **Segmentation:** Segment your email list based on interests or engagement levels to send targeted promotions of evergreen content.

Social Media Promotion

1. **Regular Sharing:** Schedule regular posts on your social media profiles to promote evergreen videos.
2. **Engagement Tactics:** Encourage followers to share your content and engage with comments and questions.

Paid Promotion

1. **YouTube Ads:** Consider running YouTube ads to promote your evergreen content to a targeted audience.
2. **Social Media Ads:** Use platforms like Facebook or Instagram to promote evergreen videos with affiliate links.

---

5. Optimizing Evergreen Content Performance

Analytics and Monitoring

1. **View Count:** Track the number of views your evergreen videos accumulate over time.
2. **Engagement Metrics:** Monitor likes, comments, shares, and watch time to gauge viewer interaction.
3. **Conversion Rate:** Analyze the conversion rate of affiliate links included in your evergreen content.

Updating and Refreshing Content

1. **Periodic Reviews:** Schedule regular reviews of evergreen content to ensure information remains accurate and relevant.
2. **Refresh Strategy:** Update outdated information, add new insights, or improve visuals and presentation to maintain viewer interest.

User Feedback and Adaptation

1. **Respond to Comments:** Engage with viewer comments and feedback to understand their needs and preferences.
2. **Content Iteration:** Use viewer insights to iterate on your content strategy and create more impactful evergreen videos.

---

6. Examples of Successful Evergreen Content

How-to Guide: Setting Up a Home Office

Title: "Ultimate Guide to Setting Up a Productive Home Office"
Content Overview:

- Introduction to the importance of a well-designed home office
- Step-by-step instructions on selecting furniture, lighting, and equipment
- Tips for maximizing productivity and comfort in a home office environment
- Conclusion with recommendations for products and resources

Product Review: Best Smartphones for Photography

Title: "Top 5 Smartphones for Amazing Photography: 2024 Edition"
Content Overview:
- Detailed review of each smartphone's camera features, performance, and user interface
- Side-by-side comparison of photo quality, video capabilities, and editing tools
- Pros and cons of each smartphone for photography enthusiasts
- Conclusion with recommendations based on different photography needs

Educational Content: Beginner's Guide to Investing

Title: "Investing 101: A Beginner's Guide to Building Wealth"
Content Overview:

- Introduction to basic investment principles, risk management, and financial goals
- Overview of different investment options, including stocks, bonds, and mutual funds
- Step-by-step instructions on creating an investment portfolio and monitoring performance
- Conclusion with tips for long-term financial planning and recommended investment platforms

---

Conclusion

Creating evergreen content is a strategic approach to building a sustainable affiliate marketing presence on YouTube. By focusing on timeless topics, optimizing for SEO, and consistently promoting your content, you can attract a steady stream of viewers and generate reliable affiliate income over the long term. Implement the strategies outlined in this guide to effectively plan, produce, promote, and optimize evergreen content that resonates with your audience and drives ongoing success for your channel.

CHAPTER NO. 9

Optimize SEO: Use relevant keywords and phrases in your video titles, descriptions, and tags to improve visibility and attract organic traffic.

To effectively optimize SEO (Search Engine Optimization) for your YouTube videos, it's essential to understand how to use relevant keywords and phrases strategically in your video titles, descriptions, and tags. SEO optimization on YouTube not only improves visibility but also helps attract organic traffic from search results and suggested videos. This comprehensive guide will cover everything you need to know about optimizing SEO for YouTube videos, with detailed strategies, best practices, and examples to help you maximize your video's reach and impact.

---

1. Understanding SEO for YouTube

What is SEO for YouTube?

SEO for YouTube involves optimizing your video content to rank higher in YouTube's search results and increase visibility to your target audience. This includes using relevant keywords, optimizing video metadata (titles, descriptions, tags), improving engagement metrics, and attracting views through organic search.

Why is SEO Important on YouTube?

1. **Increased Visibility:** Higher rankings in YouTube search results mean more visibility to potential viewers.
2. **Organic Traffic:** Optimized videos attract organic traffic from search queries and suggested videos.
3. **Audience Targeting:** Using the right keywords helps target specific audience segments interested in your content.
4. **Long-Term Benefits:** Well-optimized videos can continue to drive traffic and views over time, providing long-term benefits.

---

2. Keyword Research for YouTube

Importance of Keyword Research

Keyword research is crucial for understanding what terms and phrases your target audience is searching for on YouTube. It helps you identify high-volume keywords with low competition, optimizing your chances of ranking higher in search results.

Steps to Conduct Keyword Research

1. **Identify Seed Keywords:** Start with broad keywords related to your video topic.
2. **Use Keyword Tools:** Utilize tools like YouTube Search Suggestions, Google Keyword Planner, SEMrush, or TubeBuddy to find relevant keywords and their search volumes.
3. **Analyze Competitors:** Study top-ranking videos in your niche to see which keywords they are using.
4. **Long-Tail Keywords:** Include specific, longer phrases that are less competitive but highly relevant to your content.

Example:
If your video is about "best smartphones under $500":
- **Seed Keywords:** smartphones, best smartphones, budget smartphones

- **Long-Tail Keywords:** best smartphones under $500, top budget smartphones 2024, affordable smartphones with good camera

Tools for Keyword Research:
- **YouTube Search Suggestions:** Type your main keyword into the YouTube search bar to see autocomplete suggestions.
- **Google Keyword Planner:** Provides data on search volumes and competition for keywords.
- **SEMrush:** Offers comprehensive keyword research tools tailored for YouTube.
- **TubeBuddy:** YouTube-certified browser extension with keyword research capabilities.

---

3. Optimizing Video Titles for SEO

Best Practices for Video Titles

1. **Include Primary Keyword:** Place your primary keyword at the beginning of the title for better visibility.
2. **Be Descriptive and Compelling:** Clearly describe what your video is about to attract clicks.

3. **Keep it Concise:** Aim for titles that are concise yet informative, typically under 60 characters.
4. **Add Emotional Triggers:** Use emotional triggers like "How-to," "Ultimate Guide," "Top 10," to attract interest.

Example:
- **Before:** "Best Smartphones"
- **Optimized Title:** "Top 5 Best Smartphones Under $500 (2024) | Budget Phone Reviews"

Avoid: Titles that are overly generic or misleading, as they can lead to lower engagement and click-through rates.

---

4. Crafting Video Descriptions for SEO

Components of a Well-Optimized Description

1. **Include Keywords Naturally:** Incorporate relevant keywords and phrases throughout the description, especially in the first 100-150 characters.
2. **Provide a Summary:** Briefly summarize the content of your video to give viewers an overview.

3. **Include Timestamps:** If your video covers multiple topics, add timestamps with keywords to improve user experience and SEO.
4. **Call-to-Action (CTA):** Encourage viewers to take action, such as subscribing, liking, or visiting your website.
5. **Links and Social Media:** Include links to relevant websites or social media profiles to drive traffic.

Example:
- **Description:** "Discover the top 5 best smartphones under $500 in 2024! We review budget-friendly phones with great camera quality and performance. Timestamps: 0:00 Introduction, 1:20 Phone A Review, 2:45 Phone B Comparison. Click here to subscribe for more tech reviews!"

---

5. Optimizing Video Tags for SEO

Purpose of Video Tags

Video tags help YouTube understand the context of your video and improve its discoverability. They also play a role in suggesting related videos to viewers.

Tips for Using Video Tags

1. **Include Relevant Keywords:** Use a mix of broad and specific tags related to your video content.
2. **Use Long-Tail Tags:** Incorporate longer phrases and variations of your primary keywords.
3. **Tag Priority:** Place more important tags (primary keywords) at the beginning of your tag list.
4. **Tag Limit:** Use up to 10-12 relevant tags per video to maintain relevance without keyword stuffing.

Example:
- **Tags:** smartphones under $500, best budget phones 2024, affordable smartphones, phone reviews, budget tech gadgets, top mobiles under 500, smartphone buying guide

Avoid: Using irrelevant tags or excessive repetition of tags, as it can lead to penalties from YouTube.

---

6. Uploading and Publishing Your Video

Metadata Optimization Process

1. **Upload Settings:** Set your video privacy, category, and other basic settings before publishing.
2. **Title, Description, and Tags:** Use the optimized title, description, and tags prepared earlier.
3. **Thumbnail:** Choose an engaging thumbnail that accurately represents your video content and attracts clicks.
4. **Cards and End Screens:** Utilize YouTube's cards and end screens to promote related videos, playlists, or external links.
5. **Transcriptions and Closed Captions:** Provide accurate transcriptions or closed captions to improve accessibility and SEO.

Scheduling and Promotion

1. **Publishing Time:** Publish your video when your target audience is most active to maximize initial views and engagement.
2. **Social Sharing:** Share your video on social media platforms and relevant online communities to drive initial traffic.
3. **Engagement Strategies:** Respond to comments, encourage likes and shares, and interact with your audience to boost engagement metrics.

---

7. Analyzing and Refining Your SEO Strategy

Measuring Success with Analytics

1. **YouTube Analytics:** Monitor metrics such as views, watch time, CTR, and audience retention to assess your video's performance.
2. **Traffic Sources:** Identify where your traffic is coming from (search, suggested videos, external sites) to refine your promotion strategy.
3. **Conversion Tracking:** Track conversions from your affiliate links or other call-to-actions to measure the media's impact on your goals.

Optimizing Based on Data

1. **Identify High-Performing Keywords:** Focus on keywords that drive the most views and engagement.
2. **Content Iteration:** Create similar videos or update existing ones based on successful keywords and topics.
3. **Continuous Improvement:** Use insights from analytics to refine your SEO strategy and content creation process over time.

---

8. Examples of Well-Optimized Videos

Example 1: Tech Review

Title: "Best Laptops for Students Under $500 | Top Budget Picks 2024"

Description: "Looking for affordable laptops for school? Check out our review of the top 5 budget laptops under $500 with great performance and features! Timestamps: 0:00 Introduction, 1:20 Laptop A Review, 2:45 Laptop B Comparison. Subscribe for more tech reviews!"

Tags: laptops under 500, budget laptops 2024, student laptops, affordable tech, laptop reviews, cheap computers

Example 2: Beauty Tutorial

Title: "Natural Makeup Tutorial for Beginners | Easy Step-by-Step Guide 2024"

Description: "Learn how to create a natural makeup look with our easy tutorial for beginners! We use affordable products and share tips for flawless results. Timestamps: 0:00 Introduction, 1:20 Foundation Application, 2:45 Eye Makeup Techniques. Subscribe for more beauty tutorials!"

Tags: natural makeup tutorial, beginner makeup tips, affordable beauty products, easy makeup guide, makeup for beginners, natural cosmetics

---

Conclusion

Optimizing SEO for YouTube involves strategic use of keywords in titles, descriptions, and tags to improve visibility and attract organic traffic. By conducting thorough keyword research, crafting optimized metadata, and analyzing performance metrics, you can enhance your video's reach and engagement. Implementing these SEO best practices consistently and refining your approach based on analytics will help you build a strong presence on YouTube and achieve long-term success with your content.

To effectively optimize SEO (Search Engine Optimization) for your YouTube videos, it's essential to understand how to use relevant keywords and phrases strategically in your video titles, descriptions, and tags. SEO optimization on YouTube not only improves visibility but also helps attract organic traffic from search results and suggested videos. This comprehensive guide will cover everything you need to know about optimizing SEO for

YouTube videos, with detailed strategies, best practices, and examples to help you maximize your video's reach and impact.

CHAPTER NO. 10

Engage with Your Audience: Building a Loyal Community in YouTube Affiliate Marketing

Introduction

Engaging with your audience is not just a task but a crucial strategy for success in YouTube affiliate marketing. By fostering a loyal community through active interaction, responding to comments, addressing viewer queries, and soliciting feedback, you not only enhance viewer satisfaction but also build trust and credibility. This comprehensive guide explores various methods and best practices to effectively engage with your audience on

YouTube, ultimately refining your affiliate marketing strategies for sustainable growth.

---

1. Importance of Audience Engagement

Building Trust and Credibility

1. **Personal Connection:** Engaging with your audience creates a personal connection, making viewers feel valued and heard.
2. **Building Authority:** Consistent interaction demonstrates expertise and authority in your niche, enhancing credibility.
3. **Enhanced Brand Loyalty:** A loyal community is more likely to support your affiliate recommendations and share your content.

Driving Conversions

1. **Increased Click-through Rates (CTRs):** Actively engaging with viewers can lead to higher CTRs on affiliate links mentioned in your videos.

2. **Encouraging Action:** Responding to queries and providing additional information can prompt viewers to explore affiliate products.
3. **Word-of-Mouth Marketing:** Engaged viewers are more likely to recommend your channel and affiliate links to others, expanding your reach organically.

Feedback and Improvement

1. **Insight into Audience Preferences:** Feedback from engaged viewers helps you understand their needs and preferences better.
2. **Content Refinement:** Use feedback to refine your content strategy, creating more relevant and valuable videos.
3. **Continuous Improvement:** By addressing viewer suggestions, you can continuously improve your affiliate marketing approach.

---

2. Strategies for Effective Audience Engagement

Responding to Comments

1. **Timely Responses:** Aim to respond promptly to comments to show viewers that you value their input.
2. **Personalized Responses:** Address commenters by name and personalize your responses to demonstrate genuine interest.
3. **Encourage Further Engagement:** Ask questions or seek opinions to encourage viewers to continue the conversation.

Addressing Viewer Queries

1. **FAQ Videos:** Create videos that address frequently asked questions about products or topics in your niche.
2. **In-Video Responses:** Address specific viewer queries in future videos, acknowledging the viewer who asked the question.
3. **Direct Responses:** Respond directly to queries in the comments section, providing detailed information or directing them to relevant resources.

Soliciting Feedback

1. **Feedback Requests:** Encourage viewers to provide feedback on your content, affiliate products, or overall channel experience.

2. **Polls and Surveys:** Use YouTube's polling feature or external surveys to gather structured feedback from your audience.
3. **Implementing Feedback:** Act on constructive feedback to improve video quality, content relevance, and overall viewer satisfaction.

---

3. Techniques for Engaging Content Creation

Interactive Content Formats

1. **Q&A Sessions:** Host live Q&A sessions to interact with viewers in real-time and address their queries.
2. **Challenges and Contests:** Create challenges or contests related to your niche to encourage participation and engagement.
3. **Collaborations:** Collaborate with other influencers or experts in your niche to create diverse and engaging content.

Storytelling and Narratives

1. **Personal Stories:** Share personal anecdotes related to your affiliate products or experiences to connect emotionally with your audience.
2. **Customer Testimonials:** Showcase customer testimonials or success stories to build trust and credibility.
3. **Case Studies:** Present detailed case studies demonstrating how affiliate products have benefited users.

Call-to-Actions (CTAs)

1. **Clear and Direct CTAs:** Encourage viewers to engage with your content or affiliate links through clear CTAs.
2. **Varied CTAs:** Use different types of CTAs, such as subscribing, liking, commenting, or visiting affiliate links, to diversify viewer actions.
3. **Placement and Visibility:** Strategically place CTAs throughout your videos, in descriptions, and during interactive elements to maximize engagement.

---

4. Leveraging YouTube Features for Engagement

Community Tab

1. **Announcements and Updates:** Use the Community tab to share channel updates, new video announcements, or upcoming events.
2. **Polls and Questions:** Post polls or ask questions to directly engage with your audience and gather feedback.
3. **Exclusive Content:** Provide sneak peeks or exclusive content to Community tab subscribers to reward loyal viewers.

Live Streaming

1. **Real-Time Interaction:** Host live streams to interact with viewers in real-time, answering questions and discussing affiliate products.
2. **Q&A Sessions:** Conduct dedicated Q&A sessions during live streams to address viewer queries and provide insights.
3. **Product Demonstrations:** Showcase affiliate products live, demonstrating their features and benefits to engage potential buyers.

Comments and Replies

1. **Replying and Pinning Comments:** Reply to comments promptly and consider pinning insightful or popular comments to encourage further discussion.
2. **Moderating Comments:** Monitor and moderate comments to maintain a positive and respectful community environment.
3. **Engaging with Criticism:** Address constructive criticism professionally, using it as an opportunity to improve and clarify.

---

5. Integrating Audience Feedback into Affiliate Marketing Strategies

Analyzing Viewer Data

1. **YouTube Analytics:** Use YouTube Analytics to track viewer engagement metrics such as watch time, likes, comments, and shares.
2. **Affiliate Link Performance:** Analyze CTRs and conversion rates of affiliate links to understand which products resonate most with your audience.
3. **Demographic Insights:** Gain insights into viewer demographics to tailor your content and affiliate recommendations accordingly.

Iterative Content Optimization

1. **Content Themes:** Identify popular content themes or topics based on viewer engagement data to guide future video creation.
2. **A/B Testing:** Experiment with different content formats, titles, and CTAs to optimize engagement and conversion rates.
3. **Continuous Learning:** Stay updated with industry trends and viewer preferences to adapt your affiliate marketing strategies proactively.

Long-Term Relationship Building

1. **Subscriber Engagement:** Cultivate long-term relationships with subscribers through consistent and valuable content delivery.
2. **Subscriber Benefits:** Offer exclusive benefits to subscribers, such as early access to videos, special discounts on affiliate products, or behind-the-scenes content.
3. **Community Events:** Organize virtual meetups, webinars, or offline events to foster deeper connections with your audience and strengthen brand loyalty.

---

6. Case Studies and Examples of Effective Audience Engagement

Case Study: Tech Review Channel

Approach:
- **Interactive Q&A Sessions:** Hosted monthly live Q&A sessions to address viewer queries about tech gadgets and software.
- **Feedback Integration:** Acted on viewer feedback to improve video quality and provide more in-depth product comparisons.
- **Collaborations:** Collaborated with tech influencers to broaden the channel's reach and engage with new audiences.

Results:
- **Increased Subscriber Engagement:** Saw a 30% increase in subscriber interactions and comments on videos.
- **Higher CTRs:** Achieved a 25% increase in CTRs on affiliate links featured in comparison videos.
- **Enhanced Brand Loyalty:** Developed a loyal community of tech enthusiasts who actively recommended the channel to others.

Example: Beauty Vlogger

Approach:
- **Personalized Responses:** Responded to every comment with personalized tips and product recommendations.
- **Weekly Polls:** Conducted weekly polls on skincare concerns and product preferences to gather viewer insights.
- **Product Trials:** Tried and reviewed affiliate products based on viewer suggestions and feedback.

Results:
- **Improved Engagement Metrics:** Doubled the number of comments and shares on beauty tutorials and skincare routines.
- **Increased Affiliate Sales:** Achieved a 40% increase in affiliate sales through personalized product recommendations and endorsements.
- **Community Growth:** Expanded the channel's subscriber base by 50% through word-of-mouth recommendations and social media shares.

Conclusion

Engaging with your audience on YouTube is not just about building numbers; it's about cultivating meaningful relationships that drive mutual benefit. By actively responding to comments, addressing viewer queries, soliciting feedback, and integrating audience insights into your affiliate marketing strategies, you can foster a loyal community that supports your channel and affiliate endeavors. Continuously refine your engagement tactics, experiment with new approaches, and prioritize viewer satisfaction to sustain long-term growth and success in YouTube affiliate marketing.

Contact Us for Personalized Guidance on Earning Money Online

Thank you for reading! If you're eager to explore further opportunities in earning money online and would like personalized guidance every step of the way, don't hesitate to reach out. Whether you're navigating affiliate marketing, exploring new avenues in digital entrepreneurship, or seeking advice on maximizing your online presence, I'm here to help.

For one-on-one guidance from Ragini, feel free to contact us at

E-MAIL - meehicollection@gmail.com

PHONE NO. - 8080373872

Wishing you success and prosperity in your online ventures!

Warm regards,
Ragini

www.ingramcontent.com/pod-product-compliance
Lightning Source LLC
Chambersburg PA
CBHW082236220526
45479CB00005B/1251